Contents

The Renaissance

Renaissance artists painted realistic people, animals, landscapes, and buildings in order to create the illusion that their paintings were real worlds. These paintings show real Renaissance people and things that happened to them, as well as Christian stories and myths.

Time of Rebirth

The Renaissance, which lasted from about 1300 to 1600, was a time of great change in Europe. The term "Renaissance" means "rebirth" in French. During the Renaissance, artists and **scholars** looked back more than 1,000 years to the ideas and discoveries of ancient Rome and Greece, when the arts and sciences flourished. They wanted to recreate the greatness of these ancient civilizations and outdo them in painting, sculpture, architecture, music, theater, biology, physics, and astronomy.

Explorers circled the globe searching for new lands and inventors built new machines, such as the

printing press, which made many copies of books, rather than have scribes copy the books slowly and carefully by hand. With the printing press, the ideas of Renaissance scholars spread quickly, so that by the 1500s, the Renaissance had reached other parts of Europe, including Germany, France, England, Belgium, and the Netherlands.

Ancient Ruins

The Renaissance began in Italy, where ancient Roman sculptures lay half-buried in the ground and where the ruins of ancient Roman temples still stand. People in the Middle Ages, the period of time before the Renaissance, ignored the crumbling ruins of the Roman empire. They grazed cows in the grass that grew around them and **ransacked** the remains, looking for stone and other materials to reuse in new buildings.

The ancient ruins that inspired many Renaissance thinkers to study ancient Greek and Roman ideas, such as the ruins of the Forum in Rome, Italy, still stand today.

Painting
in the
Renaissance

UNA D'ELIA

 Crabtree Publishing Company
www.crabtreebooks.com

Renaissance World

For Lucy and Zoe

Author: Una D'Elia
Editor-in-Chief: Lionel Bender
Editors: Lynn Peppas, Simon Adams
Proofreader: Crystal Sikkens
Project coordinator: Robert Walker
Photo research: Susannah Jayes
Design concept: Robert MacGregor
Designer: Malcolm Smythe
Production coordinator: Margaret Amy Salter
Production: Kim Richardson
Prepress technician: Margaret Amy Salter

With thanks to First Folio.

Cover photo: Renaissance painter Sofonisba Anguissola's
  self-portrait from 1556.

Photo on page 1: The Mona Lisa, painted by Leonardo
  da Vinci around 1503–05.

This book was produced for Crabtree Publishing Company
  by Bender Richardson White.

Photographs and reproductions:
The Art Archive: Scrovegni Chapel, Padua/Gianni
  Dagli Orti: pages 6; Musée du Louvre, Paris/Alfredo
  Dagli Orti: page 8; Palazzo Ducale, Urbino/Alfredo
  Dagli Orti: page 12; National Gallery/Eileen Tweedy:
  pages 13, 24; Vatican Museum, Rome: page 16;
  Museo Civico, Sansepolcro/Alfredo Dagli Orti:
  page 18; Galleria degli Uffizi Florence/Alfredo
  Dagli Orti: page 19; Accademia, Venice/Alfredo
  Dagli Orti: page 21
Self portrait, 1556 by Sofonisba Anguissola
  (c.1532-1625), Muzeum Zamek, Lancut, Poland/
  The Bridgeman Art Library: cover
Corbis: Ali Meyer: page 11; Francis G Mayer: page 14;
  Arte & Immagini srl: page 15; © The Gallery
  Collection: page 20; Alinari Archives: page 22;
  Dennis Marsico: page 31
Istockphoto.com: pages 4, 10
Topfoto: pages 17, 26, 27, 28, 29, 30; Alinari: pages 5, 7;
  OM: page 9; Luisa Ricciarini: pages 1, 23; © Print
  Collector/HIP: page 25

Library and Archives Canada Cataloguing in Publication

D'Elia, Una Roman, 1973-
    Painting in the Renaissance / Una D'Elia.

(Renaissance world)
Includes index.
ISBN 978-0-7787-4592-1 (bound).--ISBN 978-0-7787-4612-6 (pbk.)

    1. Painting, Renaissance--Juvenile literature. I. Title. II. Series:
Renaissance world (St. Catharines, Ont.)

ND170.D45 2009   j759.03   C2008-907900-0

Library of Congress Cataloging-in-Publication Data

D'Elia, Una Roman, 1973-
   Painting in the Renaissance / Una D'Elia.
       p. cm. -- (Renaissance world)
   Includes index.
   ISBN 978-0-7787-4612-6 (pbk. : alk. paper) -- ISBN 978-0-7787-4592-1
(reinforced library binding : alk. paper)
   1. Painting, Renaissance--Juvenile literature. I. Title. II. Series.

ND170.D45 2009
759.03--dc22

                                                                    2008052600

Crabtree Publishing Company
www.crabtreebooks.com   1-800-387-7650

Published in Canada
Crabtree Publishing
616 Welland Ave.
St. Catharines, Ontario
L2M 5V6

Published in the United States
Crabtree Publishing
PMB16A
350 Fifth Ave., Suite 3308
New York, NY 10118

Published in the United Kingdom
Crabtree Publishing
White Cross Mills
High Town, Lancaster
LA1 4XS

Published in Australia
Crabtree Publishing
386 Mt. Alexander Rd.
Ascot Vale (Melbourne)
VIC 3032

Renaissance artists and scholars considered the ruined buildings and sculptures to be precious treasures from the past. They studied ancient works of art, and searched out old manuscripts in which they read about the lives of the Romans and Greeks.

Art and Life

Art during the Renaissance was both beautiful and practical. Renaissance artists painted on the walls and ceilings of churches, palaces, and the homes of wealthy people, as well as on wooden panels, canvases, and furniture. The rich bought silk **tapestries**, statues for their gardens, silver and gold jewelry and tableware, carved and painted furniture, painted portraits of themselves and their families, and elegantly handpainted books. Even people who were not very wealthy

Artists in the Renaissance began to show scenes from everyday life, such as this detail from a larger painting showing a game using **tarot** *cards. They produced everything from expensive paintings to cheap playing cards.*

owned works of art, such as printed playing cards, painted pots, and small religious statues. They came into daily contact with art as they washed their clothes in fountains designed by famous sculptors and walked past newly built and architectually beautiful palaces, public buildings, and churches.

TIMELINE

1290s: Giotto begins to change art by painting realistic people

1410: Filippo Brunelleschi, Italian architect, uses mathematical formulas to create **perspective**

1427: Masaccio creates depth using perspective in his frescoes

1436: Jan van Eyck, Flemish painter, is one of the first to use oil paints and glazes

1485: Sandro Botticelli paints the *Birth of Venus*

1495–98: Leonardo da Vinci paints *The Last Supper*

1503: Leonardo da Vinci paints the *Mona Lisa*

1508–12: Michelangelo paints the frescoes on the ceiling of the Sistine Chapel, a chapel in the Vatican, Rome

1511: Raphael paints the *School of Athens*, linking Italian culture with that of ancient Greece

1543: Andreas Vesalius publishes his book on human **anatomy** including accurate printed images by highly trained artists

1550: Giorgio Vasari publishes *Lives of the Most Eminent Italian Architects, Painters, and Sculptors*

Patronage

During the Renaissance, art was big business. Patrons, who included the church, rulers, bankers, merchants, and other wealthy people, hired artists to create paintings, sculptures, furniture, and other works of art for them to display in their grand houses, churches, or other public buildings.

Why Buy Art?

Patrons commissioned paintings to show their wealth and power, display their education and taste, remember their families and other loved ones, and to inspire prayer. Patrons also supported the arts by establishing academies, or schools, where artists attended **lectures** on subjects such as anatomy, geometry, and **optics**.

On the left of his painting, The Last Judgment, *Giotto showed orderly rows of saved people floating in the air, while on the right, he painted naked, twisted sinners being tormented by rivers of burning fire and many monstrous demons.*

Contracts

A patron and artist usually signed a contract, which stated how much the artist would be paid, what the subject of the painting would be, what materials would be used, how long it would take to complete the painting, and what size the finished work would be.

A contract often included a sketch of the painting as well as other details, giving the patron a good idea of what the finished work would look like.

Disagreements

Even with contracts, artists and patrons sometimes disagreed. One of the sharpest arguments was between two fierce and difficult men: the famous painter, sculptor, and architect Michelangelo Buonarotti and Pope Julius II, head of the Roman Catholic Church from 1503 to 1513 and a great patron of the arts. Michelangelo dared to disagree many times with the powerful pope about which artworks he would make and how they should be done. The artist stormed away from Rome and did not want to return,

The patron of this work, a wealthy businessman named Leonardo Buonafede, ran screaming from the painting because he thought that Rosso had painted the saints to look like scary devils. He paid for the work anyway, but put it in a tiny church in a small town, where he did not have to look at it.

but Pope Julius II forced him to come back and paint the ceiling of the Sistine Chapel, a chapel in the official residence of the pope. This became Michelangelo's most famous work. It took him four years to finish. In the end the entire ceiling was covered in 40 scenes from the Bible.

Saved by Painting

In 1305, Enrico Scrovegni commissioned the artist Giotto to paint a scene of the Last Judgment, the moment when, according to Christians, God decides who has been a good person and goes to Heaven and who has been a sinner and goes to Hell. Enrico hoped the painting would teach Christians to be good, but he also hoped it would keep him and his father from going to Hell. Like other bankers, they lent money for interest, which the church considered a sin. Enrico is in the painting, kneeling among the saved.

The Riches of Italy

Some Renaissance painters lived and worked in the courts of kings, queens, dukes, and duchesses. It was the job of court artists to paint flattering portraits of the rulers, heroic battle scenes, ancient myths, and religious works so that their noble patrons looked beautiful, rich, sophisticated, powerful, and pious.

How the Rich Lived

Life in the court was very comfortable. Court artists were paid a salary, a specific amount of money given at regular time periods such as weekly or monthly, rather than a separate fee for each piece of work they did. They were often given splendid houses, wore expensive clothes, and feasted at banquets with musicians, writers, and other important members of the court. Court artists did not just paint. They also designed theater

sets, table decorations, carriages, floats for parades, and **lavish** displays of fireworks.

Poet and Patron

Lorenzo de' Medici, a banker and ruler of Florence, Italy, was a well-known patron of the arts. He was called "The Magnificent" and was well educated, wrote poetry, and surrounded himself with other artists. He established libraries in Florence and had famous painters Botticelli and Michelangelo in his court.

Portrait of Isabella d'Este, a great patron of the arts, by Italian painter Giovanni-Francesco Caroto. Since Isabella had little money of her own, she sold her jewelry to pay for art.

The Sculpture Garden

Lorenzo de' Medici kept a garden of ancient sculptures that Michelangelo, in his spare time, together with other young artists, would study and copy. One day, when Lorenzo was visiting the garden, he saw Michelangelo sculpting the head of a mythical creature out of marble. Lorenzo was so impressed that he invited the 15-year-old boy to move into the Medici family palace and be raised with his children. There, Michelangelo studied philosophy and literature. This education led him to become a great poet as well as a painter, sculptor, and architect. Lorenzo, however, was more successful as a patron than a ruler. After his death in 1492 his family fortunes quickly declined and they lost control of Florence.

Lorenzo de' Medici was not officially the king of Florence, which was a republic with elected officials, but he had as much power as any king and would even on special occasions dress up as a king and ride a richly decorated horse through the city.

Noble Female Patrons

Patrons were usually men, because men held most of the wealth and power during the Renaissance, but a few exceptional noble women became patrons too. Isabella d'Este was a woman of noble birth who, at the age of 17, married the much older Francesco Gonzaga, the marquis, or ruler, of the northern Italian city of Mantua. Isabella delighted in the arts. She played several musical instruments, hired a private tutor to teach her Latin literature, owned a collection of ancient and Renaissance jewels and sculptures, and commissioned portraits and paintings of religious and mythological subjects from famous artists, including Leonardo da Vinci.

Applying for a Job

At the beginning of his career, the famous Italian painter Leonardo da Vinci applied to the Duke of Milan for work as a court artist. Leonardo wrote that he could design weapons, fortifications, hydraulics, and bronze sculptures. Only at the end of this letter did he mention, as if it were not important, that he could also paint. Leonardo wanted to show that he had many skills to make himself more useful than other artists wishing to work for the duke.

Becoming a Painter

In the Renaissance, most painters were men, but a few were women. They began their training as apprentices, paying to work under established painters, called "masters." Many worked as assistants until they became masters themselves.

Life as an Apprentice

Most apprentices were boys of about 12 to 14 years of age who trained in a workshop. They lived in rooms attached to masters' workshops and, at first, did small jobs, such as cleaning up the workshops and grinding and mixing paints. They practiced drawing, learned to work with different types of paint and to copy the style of their masters. They also painted backgrounds and other less important parts of their masters' works. It could take about seven years for an artist to finish an apprenticeship.

Michelangelo Buonarotti was apprenticed to the highly successful painter and expert in fresco painting, Domenico Ghirlandaio, in his busy workshop in Florence. Later in life, however, he wanted everyone to think that he was a natural artistic genius and had needed no training, so he lied and denied ever having been an apprentice.

Odd Apprenticeship

Michelangelo's father always wanted his son to become a musician, but Michelangelo had other ideas. At the age of 13, he became an apprentice to the painter Domenico Ghirlandaio. Unlike other apprentices, Michelangelo did not have to pay for his apprenticeship. Instead, because of his great talent, he was paid by the master.

Michelangelo's first large painting was the ceiling of the Sistine Chapel, which was painted from 1508 to 1512 for Pope Julius II. Some artists who were jealous of Michelangelo hoped that the young artist would not know how to do a large fresco painting, but Michelangelo had learned all the techniques as Ghirlandaio's apprentice.

Several Skills

A workshop could make a wide variety of artistic objects, such as stained glass, pottery, sculpture, and items in metal such as gold, silver, or bronze. A master might be hired to design a building or a set for a theater. An apprentice could study not only how to become a painter but also a wide range of other skills, such as **goldsmithing**, mathematics, engineering, and architecture.

An Assistant's Work

After finishing their apprenticeships, few painters could afford to set up their own workshops, so most worked for at least a few years as assistants. They helped masters by painting backgrounds, and sometimes even the main parts of paintings. It was quite common for an assistant to paint the entire work, following a master's drawing. The master would then sign and sell the work as his own. This was acceptable at the time, since the assistant was painting the master's idea in the master's style.

Women as Painters

Female painters were mostly the daughters of painters. They were usually trained at home by their fathers, since it was not considered proper for young women to move out of their homes and join workshops. The Italian painter Sofonisba Anguissola was an exception. The daughter of a learned gentleman, Sofonisba apprenticed in a workshop, although she still lived at home, and eventually became a successful painter in Italy and Spain. Sofonisba painted self-portraits, images of her sisters, and formal portraits of the Spanish royal family.

A self-portrait of Sofonisba Anguissola at an easel in 1556. She continued to paint even after she was married and had children, which was rare at a time when most women stayed at home to take care of their families and households.

Perspective and Light

Before the Renaissance, subjects in paintings looked flat and unrealistic, not three dimensional and lifelike. Renaissance artists began using perspective and new ways of painting light to add depth to their paintings and to make their work more realistic.

Linear Perspective

Linear perspective was invented in the early 1400s in Florence, Italy. The architect Filippo Brunelleschi used mathematical formulas in two painted scenes of the city of Florence, Italy, to create perspective. His scenes were a big influence on later Renaissance artists. Linear perspective is based on the **principle** that the closer an object is, the larger it appears to the viewer. Previously, artists had just made the most important figures in the painting the largest.

Linear perspective also makes use of the illusion that parallel lines seem to meet as they get closer to the horizon. The point where the parallel lines appear to meet at the horizon is called the vanishing point. Artists would ensure all horizontal lines were directed towards the vanishing point in the painting. Another element to creating linear perspective is that the more distant objects are painted smaller and placed closer together than those closer to the viewer.

We do not know the name of the artists who painted this view, which is not of a real city but an imaginary place. It is painted in correct linear perspective, with all of the lines of the pavement and the buildings that head into the picture converging on one point, in order to create an illusion of depth.

This painting by Masaccio, from the early 1400s, uses light and shadow to add realism and emotion to the painting.

Masaccio

One of the first Renaissance artists since the ancients to use correct linear perspective and realistic light and shadow was Masaccio, from Florence. Masaccio used light to make Jesus look like a real baby, sitting on his mother's lap. Bright light on Jesus's face makes him glow and look divine. Shadow on Mary's face and the throne suggests Mary's sorrow, as if she knows that her child will later suffer. Masaccio drew the throne to make it seem as if Mary and Jesus are looming over the viewer.

Aerial Perspective

Artists also began to use **aerial** perspective. They noticed that when they looked into the distance, faraway objects appeared blue in color and less clear than closer objects. Scientists now understand that this is a result of how light travels through the atmosphere. To create this feeling in the backgrounds of their works, artists painted crisp-looking rivers, hills, trees, and buildings fading into a blue haze in the far distance.

Light and Shade

In the Renaissance, painters began using light and shade to help viewers picture the shapes of objects and to imagine what the objects would feel like. First, painters decided on the direction the light was coming from. Then, they painted all the objects facing the light as bright and painted shadows on the opposite sides. They also painted cast shadows, the shadows that the objects cast on the ground. This made painted objects and figures look real and heavy, just as though they could be touched.

Artists also used light to convey emotions, such as the cheerfulness of a bright day or the sad mystery of darkness. The use of light and shade for strong contrast is called chiaroscuro. In Italian, the word *chiaro* means "light," and *oscuro* means "dark," so chiaroscuro is a technique that uses both areas of bright light with areas of dark shadow. Works by artists such as Leonardo da Vinci and Raphael use this technique.

Religious Art

Most European paintings in the Renaissance were religious and depicted Christian scenes. Christians worship one God and believe in the divinity of Jesus Christ. Until the 1500s, the main Christian church was the Roman Catholic Church, which is led by the pope.

Uses for Christian Painting

Many people in the Renaissance did not know how to read, so looking at paintings of religious scenes was one way for them to learn about their religion. Artists painted stories from the Bible and from the lives of saints, as well as beautiful visions of Heaven and terrifying views of Hell, to teach people how to lead good lives. They painted these scenes on the walls and ceilings of churches, and on altarpieces, which are paintings on wooden panels or canvas that were placed up on altars in churches. Artists also painted smaller religious paintings, which inspired prayer in homes and monasteries.

Scenes Come to Life

Artists in the Renaissance often showed scenes of the lives of saints as if they were happening in their own towns and in their own time. This helped people feel a connection with the saints. Robert Campin's *Mérode Altarpiece* is an example of this. He even put the painting's patrons in the scene as the couple peeking in the door at Mary and the angel Gabriel.

The Mérode Altarpiece, by Flemish artist Robert Campin, shows the Annunciation, when the angel Gabriel told Mary she was pregnant with Jesus. Although Christians believed this event happened in the Middle East 1,400 years before, the figures are painted in a Belgian living room.

Other artists painted this scene, which shows the angel Gabriel telling Mary that she is pregnant with Jesus. Fra Angelico chose a simple setting and costumes, so that the friar who would pray in front of the painting would not be distracted.

Religious Attacks Against Art

Most Christians believed that paintings helped people be good, but some attacked paintings. Around 1500, a friar in Florence named Savonarola preached that Christians should be humble and not lead lavish lives, or own expensive works of art and sculpture. The famous painter, Botticelli, apparently heard Savonarola's preaching and was so inspired that he burned some of his own nonreligious pictures and painted only religious ones after that.

Religious attacks against art also took place in Northern Europe in the 1500s. At the time, some Christians felt that the church, led by the pope, had become corrupt. They decided to form their own branch of Christianity, which became known as Protestantism. Protestants believed in praying directly to God and in reading God's word in the Bible, rather than using ceremonies and art to express their devotion, as Catholics did. Protestants also feared that uneducated people might think that the paintings themselves were gods, and worship the paintings instead of worshiping God. Crowds of Protestants burst into churches, smashed works of art, and scratched out the eyes of painted figures.

Fra Angelico

Guido di Pietro, who lived in Florence in the 1400s, earned the name Fra Angelico or "angelic friar," because he lived like a saint. A master of his own shop, he gave up his income and home to become a friar and live in a monastery.

There, he painted scenes of Jesus Christ and the saints on the monastery's bedroom walls. Fra Angelico's paintings had no gold, expensive pigments, ornaments, or background details that might distract the friars from their prayers.

Walls and Ceilings

Renaissance artists painted on walls and ceilings using fresco, an ancient technique in which paint is applied to wet plaster. When the plaster dries, it forms crystals around the bits of pigment in the paint, so frescoes become part of the wall.

Preparing to Paint

"Fresco" is Italian for fresh. Renaissance artists painted in *buon fresco*, or fresh plaster. The frescoes had to be painted quickly, while the plaster was wet, so artists had to know beforehand exactly what it was they wanted to paint. The only way to correct a mistake was to chip out a section of the plaster and begin again. To prepare for a fresco, artists made many drawings of the subject. The painter then made a drawing of the whole painting, called a cartoon, which was the same size as the finished work.

From Drawings to Fresco

To transfer the image, artists placed the cartoon on the wall or ceiling, then drew over the lines with a pointed metal instrument called a stylus, pushing on the paper to create indentations in the soft plaster. Another technique was to prick tiny holes along the lines of the cartoon, then dust charcoal over the holes so that it went through the holes and formed dotted lines along the wall.

Raphael painted this fresco of the ancient Greek philosophers discussing ideas and teaching students. In the center, Plato points up to the heavens as the source for truth, whereas Aristotle points down at the ground, because he believes that we need to observe the natural world to find truth. This fresco was painted in the pope's library. The pope's books of ancient philosophy were kept below it.

Leonardo da Vinci did not want to paint his Last Supper *in fresco, which dries very quickly, since he was always changing his mind about how to pose figures in his works. He tried painting on the dried plaster instead, but almost as soon as this painting was finished, the paint started falling off the wall. Artists and conservation scientists have been working to restore it ever since.*

Using the indentations or dots as a guide, the artist painted the scene's outlines in one color. The artist then applied a fine top layer of plaster to a small part of the image, as much as he could paint in one day, while the plaster was still wet. The artist then applied the paint. Once the day's work was finished, any remaining unpainted plaster was cut away, leaving a clean edge at which to begin painting the next day.

Difficulties of Fresco

Artists had to climb up on wooden **scaffolding** to reach the high parts of walls and ceilings. They also had to endure plaster and wet paint dripping down on them, particularly when painting a ceiling. Michelangelo hated painting the ceiling of the Sistine Chapel, one of the most famous frescoes from the Renaissance. He wrote a poem in which he complained that to paint the fresco, he had to bend like a bow so that his brain rested on his back. So much plaster and paint fell on his face that he looked like a tiled floor. In a little sketch of himself next to the poem, he drew himself twisted into an extremely painful position, painting a stick-figure on a ceiling.

Paint

Paint was made of rocks, plants, or even dirt ground up into a powder to make a pigment and then mixed with water. This paint was applied to the plaster using brushes. Small brushes made of ermine tail tips glued to a wooden handle were used for fine details. Very large brushes made of hog bristles glued to a handle were used to paint large patches of color or backgrounds with few details.

Altarpieces

In the Renaissance, altarpieces were like stage sets for church ceremonies. People prayed, looking up at altarpieces for inspiration while music played, perfumed incense burned, and priests in heavily embroidered silk robes raised gold chalices filled with wine.

Patrons and Saints

Patrons paid for altarpieces in order to honor God and the saints, in particular their patron saints. Every Christian had a patron saint, who was usually the saint after whom the person was named. They believed a patron saint would help pass on a person's prayers to God. A patron saint could also be a protector of a group of people, such as travelers, children, sailors, or carpenters, or be concerned with helping things, such as animals, or creating things, such as music. Patrons also paid for altarpieces as a way to display their piety and wealth publicly.

Symbolism

Some artists used symbolism in their altarpieces. This means that a simple object can have a deeper meaning or stand for something else related to the Christian theme of the piece. For example, a candle that has been blown out can symbolize Jesus's life that was cut short by being crucified on the cross. In contrast, a candle that is lit can symbolize the presence of Jesus

watching over those in the painting. Painters such as Jan van Eyck and Robert Campin made use of symbolism in this way. In the *Mérode Altarpiece*, Campin painted a kettle of water and a towel in order to symbolize the Virgin Mary's purity.

This painting by Piero della Francesca was the central panel of a larger altarpiece. It shows the Virgin Mary, the mother of Jesus Christ, protecting people by sheltering them under her robe. The man whose face is covered by a black hood is a member of a confraternity, a religious organization whose members hid their faces so that they would not seem too proud of their acts of charity.

Making an Altarpiece

Altarpieces were made on wooden panels in Italy in the 1300s and 1400s. Often a carpenter built the panel and frame. The painter covered the panel with a fine cloth and with gesso, a plaster-like paste that makes a very smooth surface for painting.

The painter drew the scene on the gesso, usually using charcoal, and marked which areas were to be painted and which were to be covered with gold leaf, or thin pieces of real gold. The artist applied the gold leaf to the panel using a reddish sticky substance called bole. The red showed through the gold leaf, giving it a rich, warm color. The gold was carefully polished to create a shiny surface, and was scratched with fine patterns to make the light reflect more brilliantly off the surface. Sometimes, pieces of painted glass or jewels were glued to the painting, adding to its rich effect.

Tempera paint was applied last. It was made from pigments ground from rocks, dirt, charred wood, plants, and even beetles, which were the source for a common red paint. The most expensive pigment, lapis lazuli, was royal blue in color and was made from a rock found only in the mountains of Afghanistan. The ground-up pigments were boiled and mixed with egg according to complex recipes. When the paint dried, it created a hard, shiny surface.

Simone Martini painted the Annunciation, *the moment when the angel Gabriel tells Mary that she is pregnant with Jesus, on an altarpiece for Siena Cathedral. Gold leaf has been applied and then indented with punches to create complex and brilliant patterns in the gold.*

Oil Paint

In the early 1400s, painters in Flanders, which is modern-day Belgium, discovered a new medium for painting: oil paint. Oil paint is made from pigments mixed with oil rather than egg or water. The use of oil paint spread to Italy around 1500 and then all over Europe.

Advantages of Oil

Artists prefer to use oil paint because it remains wet for a long time, unlike tempera which dries very quickly. With oil, artists could change their minds, wipe off one area of their work, and repaint. Artists could also create soft shadows by painting on an earlier wet layer and letting one color bleed into the other. In addition, they could apply oil paints in thin, **translucent** layers, called glazes, so that people looking at a painting could see through one layer of color to another one underneath.

Madonna and Child with Chancellor Rolin *by Jan van Eyck painted in oil about 1435. He was one of the first artists to make use of oil paint, which became popular because it allowed artists to paint in translucent glazes and so paint deeper darks and more brilliant lights.*

Jan van Eyck

The first person who perfected the use of glazes in oil paints to create brilliant colors was Jan van Eyck, who worked in Flanders in the early 1400s. He began by making an underpainting, using a thin layer of oil paint to create shadows on white gesso. After the underpainting dried, van Eyck diluted some new oil paint with a lot of linseed oil and used this to paint over the underpaint so that it formed a glaze. The shadows of the underpaint remained visible through this glaze. Van Eyck painted many layers of glazes in different colors. Light travels through the glazes and is absorbed by the deep layers of shadow. In areas without shadows, the light reflects off the white gesso underneath so that the painting seems to glow.

Titian was working on this painting of the Virgin Mary mourning over the death of Christ for his own tomb. He died before finishing it, so the figure of Christ is still only roughly sketched out with a few quick strokes of paint. Had he finished the painting, Titian would have added more paint, not with careful fine strokes but rather with rough blobs, as he did at the end of his life.

A Mysterious Atmosphere

Leonardo da Vinci used oil paint, applied in glazes, to create soft-looking figures without sharp outlines. In paintings such as the *Mona Lisa*, illustrated on the next page, Leonardo used oil glazes to blur the edges of the figures in his paintings so that you cannot tell where the skins ends and the hair begins, and so that the hills seem to rise out of the mist. The transitions of tones across this and other paintings is so subtle and gradual that they are hardly noticed. This gives his paintings a strange and mysterious atmosphere, called *sfumato*, a word which means "smoky" in Italian.

Painting with Blobs

In the middle of the 1500s, Titian, an artist who lived and worked in Venice, Italy, decided to create paintings with an unfinished, energetic look. He began painting on rough canvas rather than on smooth wooden panels or finely woven canvas. He applied oil paint quickly with a large brush and his fingers. This left big, rough strokes on the canvas which, from close up, made the paintings look like blobs. From further away, the paintings looked more alive than carefully finished paintings.

Portraits

Before the Renaissance, portraits were very rare and were only painted of kings and other powerful people. Beginning in the 1400s, Renaissance artists painted portraits not only of great rulers but also of merchants, wealthy craftspeople, bankers, and children from rich families.

Powerful Portraits

A portrait of a powerful ruler could inspire respect or even fear in his people. Portraits could also help people remember someone who had died or was away, perhaps fighting in a war. When a king wanted to marry, he sent an artist to paint portraits of possible brides to see if they were beautiful. Not all portraits were flattering. To shame escaped criminals, the government of Florence, Italy, had artists paint, on the outside walls of public buildings, humiliating life-size portraits of criminals dangling upside-down for all to see. The wife of the writer Baldassare Castiglione owned a portrait of her husband, which was painted by Raphael. When her husband was traveling, she spoke to the portrait, imagining it was real.

Piero della Francesca painted the duke and duchess of Urbino in profile. The duke was only ever painted from this side as he had lost his right eye in a hunting accident.

Kinds of Portraits

Portraits were painted on walls, wooden panels, canvases, paper, and **vellum** with fresco, tempera, and oil. The most expensive ones were life-size portraits of the full body. Nobles also owned miniature portraits, which were sometimes no more than 1 inch (2.5 cm) wide. These were worn on a chain or as a brooch, or kept hidden as a token of a secret love.

Ideal and Real Portraits

In Italy, portraits painted in the 1400s were usually profiles, seen from the side, like the faces of Roman emperors on coins. The subjects look distant, which makes them

Sitting for Portraits

Rich and powerful people did not want to pose for hours while artists painted their portraits. Nobles usually posed for a brief time while artists made drawings of their faces. Then, the nobles lent the artists fancy clothes and suits of armor. An apprentice posed, wearing the clothes or armor, so that the artist could finish the painting when the noble was no longer there.

seem dignified and noble. In Flanders, people were painted in a three-quarter view, looking out at viewers, which makes them seem more real and friendly. To add to the realism, Flemish artists painted details such as wrinkles and the stubble on a man's chin, even though this may have made the portrait less flattering.

Leonardo da Vinci wanted to create a sense of movement in his portraits and to portray a person's thoughts. His most famous work, the *Mona Lisa*, unlike other Italian portraits of the time, has her body facing to the side with her head turned to the viewer, as if she were smiling at someone walking into the room. The movement is just a slight twist of the body and a half smile, enough to make the portrait come alive, as if she could speak.

The Mona Lisa *is probably a portrait of Lisa Gherardini, the wife of the wealthy Florentine merchant Francesco del Giocondo.*

The Human Body

Paintings made in the Middle Ages show the human body out of proportion and without the proper muscle and bone structure. In the Renaissance, artists learned to paint the human body in a newly realistic way by studying ancient statues, nude models, and anatomy.

Nudes

Unlike the Middle Ages, when people thought the body was sinful and something to hide, educated people in the Renaissance believed that a beautiful body was a sign of inner goodness. Artists painted heroes, gods, and even saints in the nude. Michelangelo painted nudes in the scenes from the Bible on the ceiling and end wall of the Sistine Chapel. Paintings of nudes were kept in the homes of wealthy patrons and even in churches. Sometimes, church officials objected to this display of nudity, particularly in religious art, so some nudes were covered with painted drapery.

Jesus Christ is wearing only a loincloth so that he can be baptized with water from the Jordan River by John the Baptist. Piero della Francesca painted Jesus with a realistic contrapposto *pose and a beautiful, almost glowing white body, to show that he is divine.*

Contrapposto

Renaissance artists tried to capture movement of the human body in their paintings rather than paint people standing stiffly, the way artists did in the Middle Ages. One pose that Renaissance painters copied from ancient statues is called *contrapposto*, which means "contrasting pose" in Italian. The *contrapposto* pose has one straight leg and one bent leg, which is more relaxed and makes figures look as if they are about to walk forward. Try standing with both legs stiff, and then with one leg bent, to see which feels more natural. The pose also involves tilting the shoulders in one direction while the hips tilt the other way. This creates a sense of movement and tension in the figure.

Botticelli created a painting of Primavera, *which means "spring" in Italian, by painting a delightful garden inhabited by mythological gods and goddesses. The three Graces, who dance on the left, and Venus, in the center, are made ideally beautiful according to Renaissance standards, with long necks, small heads, rounded bellies, and broad hips.*

Idealizing the Body

Even though artists painted the human body realistically in terms of its anatomy and position, they also exaggerated certain features to make people look more beautiful than they really were. In the 1400s, men in portraits, in mythological paintings, and in paintings of saints were all shown as being tall, slim, and graceful, which was what people considered beautiful for men at the time. In the 1500s, men were painted with bulging, exaggerated muscles to make them look like superhuman heroes.

Female Beauty

Sometimes saints and other important women were shown with huge muscles to make them look more powerful. Beautiful women of the time were thought to be tall, with pale skin, blond hair, a high forehead, soft, curving bodies, and a round belly.

Many women in paintings were portrayed with these curves, making them look impossibly beautiful. Then, as now, real women tried to make themselves look like these ideal beauties. They covered their faces with white powder, dyed their hair blond, plucked hair from their foreheads, and wore high shoes.

Human Anatomy

Andreas Vesalius wrote a seven-volume book on human anatomy in 1543. It included detailed, carefully illustrated pictures done by well-trained artists to show the human skeleton and muscles. Vesalius was also an anatomy teacher, who used illustrations in addition to words to help students understand information. He is considered the father of modern studies in human anatomy.

Everyday Life

In the Renaissance, artists painted events that happened in their own time. These paintings showed the violence of war, as well as more humble scenes from the lives of peasants.

Battles and Warriors

The Renaissance was a time of many wars. Countries did not have established borders, so rulers constantly fought for control of land. Some wars or battles were also based, at least in part, on religion. In Italy in the 1300s, cities often warred with other cities. Later, in the 1400s, when Italy became more peaceful internally, the country was attacked by France and Spain. Spain, using its fleet of warships known as the Spanish Armada, tried but failed to invade England in 1588.

Rulers, governments, and warriors had artists paint battle scenes in their houses and government buildings to show themselves as strong. Some paintings honored one war hero, while others were large battle scenes with thousands of figures and a great deal of action. Governments also had artists paint works of art to honor their mercenaries, or foreign soldiers whom they paid to fight for them. They hoped that these paintings would encourage the mercenaries to remain loyal to them and not fight for another government that offered them more money.

This scene from Paolo Uccello's Battle of San Romano, *makes use of a pattern of lances that direct the eye around the painting. The dead and the lances on the ground form a checkerboard.*

Battle Painter

Paolo Uccello was one of the most famous painters of battle scenes. In 1435, in Florence, he painted the *Battle of San Romano,* which was a series of three panels or scenes that showed a war that had been fought in 1432 between the troops of Florence and those of the nearby city of Siena. Uccello used his knowledge of perspective and human and horse anatomy to depict accurately many figures rushing at one another, some falling dead on the ground and being trampled by other soldiers.

Paintings of Peasants

In the 1500s, Protestants in northern Europe no longer wanted religious paintings, so artists began painting other subjects. Paintings of the everyday lives of peasants became popular. The artist Pieter Bruegel the Elder used to dress as a peasant and go to dances, weddings, and other celebrations to observe and sketch the people there. He painted them in the realistic situations and settings of the day, such as working in the hills. His series of paintings on the seasons show the peasants working at activities appropriate for that particular season.

Some people think Bruegel's paintings made fun of peasants by showing them as gap-toothed, big-footed fools, and that these were unfair stereotypes that wealthy people at the time had about the poor. Others think that he made clever observations about human behavior, and used the foolishness of peasants to symbolize the foolishness of humans in general.

Pieter Bruegel captures a scene at a peasant wedding. The bride is the woman near the back sitting in front of the dark wall hanging.

The Imaginary World

Even though Renaissance artists portrayed their subjects in realistic ways, they still had to use their imaginations. When painting Christian stories and ancient myths, artists had to find ways to show the supernatural, including angels, demons, and gods.

Angels and Demons

Christians believe in angels, good spirits who help Christians, and demons, evil spirits who tempt people to sin. Artists sometimes painted angels as playful fat babies, to give a sense of joy. At other times, they showed angels as adults with birds' wings, to suggest that they can soar up to Heaven. Devils and demons were shown as monsters, part human and part animal.

Mythological Paintings

Renaissance artists also painted myths, which are ancient stories about the loves, triumphs, and tragedies of Greek and Roman gods and goddesses. Mythological paintings were made to decorate the houses of the wealthy, often as part of a piece of furniture. They were painted onto the headboards of beds, the backs of benches, and on to chests, cabinets, and wall panels.

Hieronymus Bosch invented strange monsters that were scary and fascinating in his painting Garden of Earthly Delights.

Bruegel's painting, *Landscape with the Fall of Icarus,* shows the myth of proud Icarus who flew too close to the Sun with wings made of wax, despite his father's warning not to do so. The Sun melted his wings and so Icarus fell to his death. In Bruegel's scene, all we can see are Icarus's little legs poking out of the water. The setting is the decidedly real Flemish coast. Nearby, a ship sails and a peasant plows his field. No one in the painting seems to care about this tragedy. Icarus's fall is placed off to the side as opposed to the usual centralized placement given to a main event. Perhaps this is meant to show that even when one person comes to a tragic end, life goes on.

Bruegel made his painting, Landscape with the Fall of Icarus, *look like a scene of everyday life. Icarus's tiny legs, which are difficult to spot, are the only hint of the mythological story.*

Mannerism

A new style of art, called Mannerism, emerged in Italy around 1520. Mannerist paintings presented their subjects in ways that went against reality. The name comes from the Italian *maniera*, meaning "style" or "way of working."

Mannerism was a manner, or style, of painting where linear perspective and proportion are distorted and elongated. Figures were twisted to create more emotion or tension or to create an exaggerated look of elegance. People might have torsos or necks or other features that look too long.

There are abrupt jumps from foreground to background instead of a realistic, gradual transition. The confusing use of space, harsh colors, and incorrect scale challenged viewers to find meaning in the painting.

Michelangelo's *The Last Judgment*, from later in his life, is painted in this style. He shows the twisted, gruesome figures of sinners descending to Hell, which is populated by creatures from Greek mythology and from the poem *Inferno*, written by Dante Alighieri in the 1310s. The painting's unusual depiction of Hell, and the numerous nudes, caused controversy when it was revealed.

Birth of Venus

Sandro Botticelli was famous for his mythological paintings of the late 1400s. *Birth of Venus* shows Venus, the goddess of love, being born out of the sea on a large scallop shell. Wind gods blow her to shore, where an attendant waits to wrap her in a flowery cloak. To make the painting even more dreamlike, Botticelli made all the figures float in the air or stand on tiptoe, in beautiful poses like dancers.

The Rise of Art

By the end of the Renaissance, patrons were buying art not just to teach religious messages or to show their wealth or power, but because it was beautiful. They began to think of artists as creative geniuses, and displayed their work in galleries. People became fascinated with the artists' lives, so authors started writing biographies about them.

The Changing Status of the Artist

In the Middle Ages, people who made art were considered craftsmen. They did not have a great deal of education or a very high position in society. In the late 1500s, artists began studying in academies and writing theories about their art. They were considered educated people, and their social status rose. Artists signed their works to show pride in what they had done, and some became very famous.

New Kinds of Contracts

Artists' new status was evident in the contracts that they signed with their patrons. At the beginning of the Renaissance, the cost of a painting was based on the preciousness of the materials that the artist used, such as gold and expensive paints. It was less important who painted the work.

During the 1600s, Willem Van Haecht painted this view of a gallery full of Renaissance portraits, scenes from everyday life, religious paintings, and mythological scenes.

By the end of the Renaissance, the cost of a painting was based on which master would create the work of art and on how much of the painting the master, as opposed to an apprentice or assistant, would paint. In addition, for most of the Renaissance, patrons usually decided the subject of a painting. By the late 1500s, some patrons allowed artists to choose the subject. They did not care what the painting showed. They just wanted a painting by a famous artist.

New Galleries

The first art galleries appeared in the 1500s. Wealthy people began to set aside special rooms in their palaces as galleries and invited others to come and admire the art. There were portraits, landscapes, religious scenes, mythological paintings, and scenes of everyday life on small- or medium-size panels and canvases. Also on display were altarpieces, made earlier in the Renaissance, that had been cut up into separate, smaller paintings and sold to buyers. The paintings in these galleries were collected and exchanged all over Europe.

Renaissance Man

Leonardo da Vinci was a painter who was curious about so many different aspects of nature and science. He studied human anatomy, bird flight, and geology, and designed items as diverse as machine guns, movable bridges, and parachutes. He created more than 4,000 pages of notes and diagrams for his observations and ideas. Because of his wide-ranging knowledge, Leonardo has become an enduring symbol of the Renaissance.

Biographies

Renaissance biographers, people who write about someone else's life, began to focus on nonreligous people, such as artists. Giorgio Vasari, a painter and architect, first published his history of great artists, titled *Lives of the Most Eminent Italian Architects, Painters, and Sculptors*, in 1550. He wrote about Giotto, Botticelli, Leonardo, Michelangelo, and Raphael, among others. It is still one of the most important books on art history.

Today, people still like to view art in art galleries. Here a woman observes Raphael's portrait of a woman with a veil from 1516, La Velata, in the Galleria Palatina in Florence, Italy.

Further Reading and Websites

Koestler-Grack, Rachel A. *Leonardo da Vinci: Artist, Inventor, and Renaissance Man*. New York: Chelsea House Publications, 2005

Phillips, John. *Leonardo da Vinci: The Genius Who Defined the Renaissance*, National Geographic Children's Books, 2008

Somervill, Barbara A. *Michelangelo: Sculptor and Painter*. Mankato, MN: Compass Point Books, 2005

Wilkinson, Philip. *Michaelangelo: The Young Artist Who Dreamed of Perfection*. National Geographic Children's Books, 2006

Corrain, Lucia. *The Art of the Renaissance*. New York: Peter Bedrick, 2001

Fitzpatrick, Anne. *The Renaissance: Movements in Art*. Mankato, MN: Creative Education, 2005

Teacher Oz's Kingdom of History—Renaissance www.teacheroz.com/renaissance.htm

Renaissance Connection www.renaissanceconnection.org

Exhibits Collection—Renaissance www.learner.org/interactives/renaissance

Glossary

anatomy How the parts of a human, animal, or plant are arranged and work together

aerial To do with the air

chalices Cups or goblets with wide mouths often used for wine in religious ceremonies

divine Like God, also of or from God

goldsmithing The process of working with gold or making items out of gold

lavish Extravagant, expensive

lectures Long speeches given to large audiences designed to teach a specific topic

medium The material an artist uses to create art

optics The study of the eye and eyesight

perspective Drawing or painting on a flat surface to create the look of depth; a way of looking at something

pigment Powder used to give color to paint

pious Strictly following a system of religious duties and rules

principle A rule, truth, or law

proportion The measure of something compared to something else; how two things relate in size

ransacked Searched violently and destructively with the aim to steal valuable items

scaffolding Large wooden framework with platforms used to reach high places

scholars People who study to become knowledgeable; people who have learned a lot

tapestries Decorative woven fabrics usually hung on a wall or covering furniture

tarot Game of cards, or deck of cards used in fortune telling

translucent Not completely clear but still lets light through

vellum Smooth paper originally made from calf's skin

Index

Printed in the U.S.A. — CG